Writing in Spirit

Workbook

Ruth Lee, Scribe

Copyright © 2014 Ruth Lee. All rights reserved. No portion of this book may be reproduced mechanically, electronically, or by any other means, including photocopying, without written permission of the publisher. It is illegal to copy this book, post it to a website, or distribute it by any other means without permission from the publisher.

For more information about Ruth Lee and her books go to
www.ruthlee-scribe.com

Spirit Wind Books, an imprint of Love Your Life Publishing
427 N Tatnall St # 90946
Wilmington, DE 19801-2230
ISBN: 978-1-934509-76-0

Printed in the United States of America

First Printing 2014

*Dedicated to Kathleen Safchick, intrepid traveling companion,
Who never asked why or where—just started packing her bags!*

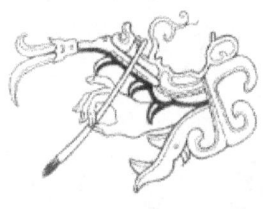

The time to begin is now...
Are you ready to write or waiting to be inspired?

Let's Begin Writing in Spirit

To enter the sacred confines of your inner being or spiritual life, start with prayer. Prayer is not as easy as many think it should be, because it requires you to settle down and empty your mind of the many things you acquire every few hours and do not bother to figure out—until you sit quietly for a few minutes or an hour.

Once seated and quiet, thoughts tend to rush about and intrude into your quietude. Do not let your thoughts confuse you now! Instead, take a deep and cleansing breath—let air spread through your chest—let oxygen fill all the crevices and seep into your heart until you feel relaxed and renewed, ready for whatever comes next.

While taking time to delve into your spiritual work, instead of what your mind set aside to do during quietude, ask for a Divine presence to visit you and emit peace. As you let such blessings enter and fill you to the uppermost region of your entire being, inhale and exhale slowly while imagining peace and love.

Once you complete this simple exercise, ask God for what you need *now*...

Thus ends your preparation for each and every scribed session
You embark upon hereafter

The urge to write may be so great that you skip setting the stage for Spirit to arrive, instead trying to force your hand to create words. Don't let your mind get carried away!

There should be no feelings of worry or confusion as you prepare to Write in Spirit. Stop thinking about whether or not you should use a pen or pencil, if you need a new journal, and other such things. Instead, relax and follow the instructions provided on the previous page. In time the procedure will become habitual and you will easily access your Spiritual Guides or Higher Self without thought.

Once ready to Write in Spirit, look at the pen or pencil you selected, let it become an extension of your inner being—acting as the force that initiates work on manuscripts designed to enlighten *your* mind.

At this point, date and dedicate your work—every time!

Always keep in mind you are a conduit of all that surrounds you—be it beauty, evil, love, hate, sincerity, deceit. You are who you are now based on choices *you* made in the past. You will change over time as a result of changes made today and every day to follow.

You are now ready to begin Writing in Spirit!

But Keep in Mind...

Whenever you put something on paper, whether using a pen, pencil, or brush, it creates inroads in your mind that over time become etched in your brain. Such thoughts change how you arrange your many lives lived within this time. Yes, you live many different lives all the time, and you are faced with others equally diverse and living at varying levels not displayed or shared with you or others.

Once you realize you are about to write about a single aspect of your entire human personality, you may assume this heightened awareness is caused by the Holy Spirit of God or in some other way expresses your spirituality, but it may not have anything to do with either.

Many times you are merely writing what is uppermost in your mind, or in some cases, your imagination—and in rare cases, that which comes through sacred channels and you cannot control the content. When speaking of *Writing in Spirit*, we are referring to the latter method of writing—fully aware most students and seekers will not achieve it.

Know now, at the beginning of your practice in this workbook, that your writing will improve and open your everyday life to new resources from within *you* and your Higher Self. You will be able to more easily create new and original material. However, you may never reach the point where you are *Writing in Spirit* as taught by Ruth Lee, Scribe.

When Ready to *Write in Spirit*...

Be still and wait for a calm state of mind or sense of peace to engulf you. Ignore any thoughts that try to interrupt your journey inward. Instead, breathe deeply, holding each breath as long as it is comfortable...then exhale slowly through your mouth without making sounds.

Do not neglect to do this simple exercise every time you wish to connect with your inner being and Write in Spirit!

As previously instructed, slip quietly into solitude of your own making—a place you may describe as *meditation*. To discourage thought, count your breaths until something clicks and you sense you have crossed a line into another time or mindset.

When you sense something changing within you, stay with it. Welcome new ideas or sensations before attempting to write anything.

As you date and dedicate your work, notice how each new entry affects your writing. Take note of subtle differences each time you write!

Before you seek to enhance your spiritual discoveries, perhaps anticipating great words of wisdom, write out the following sentence right below the date and dedication:

I am about to reveal something I wish to share with me.

Keep writing this sentence as many times as it takes until something stirs within you. When smiling and at ease, begin writing!

If your mind is not calm—perhaps upset with another or experiencing pain and sorrow, smile and continue the deep breathing exercises until you can relax and smile easily. Do not attempt to Write in Spirit until you are smiling and calm.

Use a notebook or journal reserved especially for *Writing in Spirit,* to express your inner visions or messages as they seemingly spill out onto the page without your critical mind arranging them in space and time. Do not edit or change what arrives in time!

Regardless of What You Write

You cannot possibly achieve a high state of grace if others intrude upon your faith and inner space. Your work, unless you are paid to do it, is a private matter. If anyone crowds you while writing, move or ask them to not bother you. All who respect you or have any sense of what is due others will honor your privacy whenever you write. Once settled and able to work undisturbed, write out the following commands several times:

I am happy! I am about to discover something amazing about me!

Do you now sense something new headed toward you? If so, take time to write out what you know or sense will come to be. Explain in detail what you feel about it.

If you feel strained or strange, you are not relaxed and releasing tension as it builds within your body and/or mind. When necessary, repeat the entire sequence of opening exercises until you can write without worry or concern about your personal well-being.

When sad or upset, smile. Relax and sense you can safely write about whatever is working its way through your mind at this time. Remember to breathe deeply and evenly while counting how many breaths it takes before you feel safe, content, and able to write without interruption.

Once happy, glad, or not feeling sad, let whatever comes to mind appear—then write it out in your notebook. Write as quickly as you can without passing judgment on it.

Do not hold back or edit what you write now!

Every Time You Use This Workbook...

Work on one Lesson at a time—and only one lesson on any given day! Concentrate on only one idea or theme at a time—until it becomes a daily routine.

If you should ever be unsure about what or when to write, follow this routine:
- Breathe deeply as you ease out of this reality
- Release control over your thoughts to your Divinity
- Encourage your mind to sit idle as you write
- Do not criticize or analyze what you write!

When ready to enter a brighter, lighter, more wonderful life:
- Breathe deeply and evenly
- Lower your pulse and heart rates
- Relax and let your everyday life dim and disappear
- Remember not to rush your practice!

This approach to writing develops your intuition!

In time your everyday prose and prosaic writing will display touches of wisdom and wit seldom seen in the past. However, this is not *Writing in Spirit!* You are merely accessing *The Writer* who resides within us all. This is necessary if you wish to write for others.

When you wish to Write in Spirit, you need at least 5-10 minutes of uninterrupted mindfulness or meditation before attempting to open the inner lines to your Higher Self. In time you may aspire to write without interruption for hours at a time, but do not expect to Write in Spirit for lengthy periods until you can easily maintain deep breathing and remain in an altered state of mind throughout. These periods should not exceed your ability to be happy, content, and physically relaxed while writing.

Be aware some individuals at some point may develop and grow to such heights spiritually that the Holy Spirit may call upon them and ask for their help in reaching others through their writing. Such individuals are known as Spiritual Scribes. We are not attempting to prepare you for such work. That is far beyond the power of teachers such as we, Teachers of the Higher Planes, to create such a curriculum. Indeed, we seek out *spiritual scribes* here and now to publish *our* works on Earth.

Let your Writing in Spirit begin now!

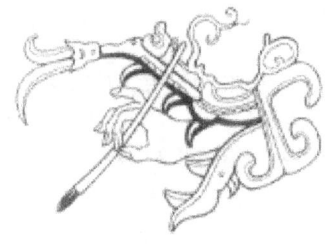

Lesson One

Can you lower your heart rate by picking up a pen?
Do you feel wonderful?
If so, you are ready to begin Writing in Spirit!

With pen in hand, begin writing a letter to someone you wish to communicate with today. Write anything and everything that enters your mind, but do not force it! Sit patiently—releasing all conscious worries and concerns. Let words form unbidden and watch as your hand starts writing without any conscious thought on your part.

Your writing may appear to be somewhat automatic, thus some call it *automatic writing*. This is not to be confused with *Writing in Spirit,* which usually develops only after much practice. At times some seemingly skip this phase and begin to easily Write in Spirit. Good for you if you can, but no worry if instead you write *automatically* and words pouring across the page reveal feelings or emotions you recognize but seldom vocalize or express.

When ready to earnestly begin your first *Writing in Spirit* practice session, copy the following exercise into your notebook, filling in the blanks as you go.

Ruth Lee

Dear New, Improved Me...

Today begins a new chapter in my everyday world and inner life. I still feel and look the same to everyone who knows or greets me, but I am about to change. I have a desire to change and will start by _____

Once I complete this first step, I will integrate it into my everyday life by _____

When I do it easily and happily, I intend to tell everyone _____
_____

Today brings a new view of others. The first person I wish to meet is _____

If possible, I hope to meet others of like-mind. If I do not befriend others, it's because they intentionally _____
_____

Am I too sensitive or self-involved to notice what happens around me? _____

If asked, what can you do to make life better for others or what is unnecessary to do for them? This is my response: _____
_____

If I cannot live up to my fullest potential, I believe this is the reason:
_____

While remaining true to me, how can I please others? _____
_____

When happy I feel better! I'm more able to cope, but I'm seldom happy when: _____

This always makes me smile _____
_____

The best adjective to describe 'me' now is:
_____

I thank all in Spirit for listening to me complain, applaud, or write whatever came into my mind during this time together.

Sincerely,
The Old Me

Note: Whenever blocked or stuck—unable to Write in Spirit—return to this exercise and rework it.

Consider this work as a moment in time when you embraced peace and silence within your mind—possibly meditating at a deeper level than ever before. However, if you could not write in private or trust the wisdom of your Higher Self, regard this exercise as merely an introduction to *Writing in Spirit* and assign more time to practice it again.

Spirit will find you when you are ready to write!

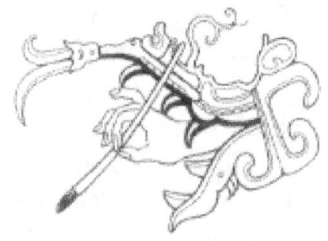

Lesson Two

What is your first lesson as a writer? You must write...or perish without having mastered your art and the ability to easily connect with your inner being, as you do when *Writing in Spirit*. Even if you think you are not ready to Write in Spirit, begin writing immediately and complete this assignment in one sitting. Work hard to remove all doubt, so you can write non-stop in the days to follow.

This class is about persistence and why it is required—regardless of what you may aspire to do this life. You cannot succeed by trying something once and giving up because it was not as easy as you thought it would be. That is vanity, and writers cannot afford to indulge such petty ideas. Dabbling, instead of applying yourself to what you wish to accomplish, is foolish—certainly not what *writers* tolerate or teach others. To produce your best work you must apply yourself to writing and do it a lot!

You are now entering the mind of a *writer*, and that writer is asking for help in designing a new kind of work for you to follow and master. You may achieve the ability to write as you wish, yet no one gets it—or everyone says 'it's great' without understanding why you felt compelled to share it. It is important that you appreciate your work and not be bothered when others do not.

This class is presided over by one who has written more words than you will ever write if just starting to write and are over the age of 48. You cannot surpass Ruth Lee's abundance of work and output on Earth, but she is willing to help you grow and match your work to hers.

As you may sense by now, this is a grand and glorious plan—not the usual kind of workbook where you write, then set it aside and never bother working with it again. You may believe you can drop out and no one would ever know—but YOU will know! Do not let your mind lead all the time, thus never connect with your Higher Guides or Higher Self while in this life.

Today you may demonstrate a bit of resistance and a lot of romantic ideas about how easy it must be to let your Higher Self write while you sit and do little. That is not how it is! You will be shocked if you expect that to be the case. Instead, sense that even copying in cursive script what is printed here, thus not so easy-to-read and forget, you learn more than those who read only and never bother to write it out. With this in mind, rewrite every word of this lesson in any lined notebook you choose to use.

Note: *It is important to honor your writing—even your practice exercises. Establish set guidelines you will follow and use daily. It also helps to maintain a special notebook for Writing in Spirit, rather than combining such work with your dream interpretations or diary.*

Lesson Three

Your work is improving, yet you have done what anyone else could easily do, too. Can it be everyone writes alike? Do you believe you are unique? What would it take to make you a better writer than all others? That is how the ego thinks and wishes to work. It does not approve of time spent working for others or for no money.

By now you can see if you did not complete Lesson One and are trying to leap ahead of everyone else, that you are stuck. You have not gained an inch of print on those who consistently followed through and completed each assignment as given. Thus you feel pressure from working hard following another's art. Would you try to paint without studying what others have done?

Begin each session with the assumption you have something wise to do and wish to know what it is, and hopefully you will be able to share it with others. This way of working is not vain, ignorant, or lacking sense. It is not egotistical to wish to help others while you work on yourself. If you prefer to learn as you go it alone, then all you need do is meditate for the rest of this session. You have to meditate anyway, so you need never wait for us to say it is time to meditate.

Today is another class that either begins with you writing out the letter printed in Lesson One or feeling good enough to write immediately without a warm-up exercise. If you are already writing, stop! Let up while we catch up with those working hard and eager to rapidly move ahead now.

Those who have written in Spirit in the past may wish to prove they can do it now, yet find themselves stuck or unable to get out of first gear. Why would that happen? Because you are learning a method of working with Spirit you did not use in the past and are unwilling to give up your old writing methods.

Clear your mind now!

Did you feel anything happen? If so, what did you feel loosen or leave? Write about life as if you have a list of work you have been given and wish to pursue immediately. List each gift. Opposite each gift, describe what you will do with it or how much you can expect others to help you explore or buy more of whatever you crave today.

In the event you are looking for paper on which to outline this self-exploration, use the *Writing in Spirit Notebook* or pages that easily fit in a loose-leaf notebook. Score pages into tables, blocks, or columns, then label each one according to your mind's design.

Do you believe you have to work hard to develop your art? You are working hard now, or you are not *Writing in Spirit*. To work out a way to develop what some call art and others call craft, or a method of communicating with others, you must first know who you are and why you wish to star.

This is not an easy lesson for some, yet others will fly through it as if on golden wings—soaring high above the crowd. Regardless of which group you seemingly belong, describe who you are now and why you wish to fly.

Did you stop and write out your thoughts or merely pause and think? A writer prefers to put pen to paper and see what appears, but that does not mean the thinker cannot produce written art, too. You can write—or you are beginning to realize writing is hard work. Take your time, but write out a paragraph describing what you do for your art when not actually working.

Do writers draw in order to open their eyes to greater flaws in society or self or to let colors draw them into other lives? What do you like, and what drives you crazy when it is not done right?

As your mind hovers over these pages at points where you are engaged in a thought process unlike what you normally pursue, you may wonder if this means you can Write in Spirit, too...It does not!

When you can let go of everything and every thought, and transfer your mind to another place and time, you have arrived on the platform required to Write in Spirit where you receive work and support from those you worked with before—even if you do not believe you could ever access such information.

The spiritual platform we see and believe you can achieve will be easy for one and difficult for many others. You either believe you can Write in Spirit now or take the entire year ahead to achieve it. Which is it to be?

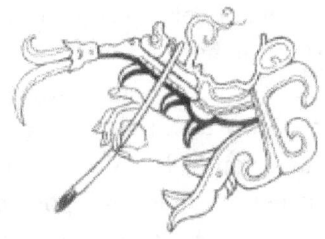

Lesson Four

Can you see a new being when you now check your image in a mirror, or are you about the same as when you started working with us this way? If you change quickly and easily, your outer appearance may never seem to age or be different to outsiders; but if it takes years for you to access your Spiritual Guides and others who work inside your life, your appearance does not remain as it is now. That makes sense, doesn't it? Then start making your work count and forget about trying to figure it out!

As you develop enough stamina to write for several days without feeling deprived of whatever you think is absolutely necessary, you will wonder why everyone does not want to write, too. You will leap ahead and wish you could Write in Spirit constantly, learning how to handle everything that ever bothered you or you wanted to know. The danger is you will overuse your Spiritual Guides, because you want to fly and divide your time between your spiritual life and whatever you do to make a living now.

This is being said for your benefit: You cannot give up concentrating on how to improve your life in this world. Once you learn to access your inner wisdom, all this will make more sense than it does now. You will find your mind does not always want to be put aside and will interrupt *You*—your Higher Self—as you work here and now. You may find your body complaining, because it wants to move and do something new. So remember, Spirit can overcome anything that might block your work while here!

Taking all of this very seriously is the wisest way to proceed, but some play more than they are willing to pray. We care not. You do whatever you do because you feel it is worthwhile or it is something you wish to figure out before others tell you they do it or can do it better than you. For sure, you are competitive in the outer world, but you are unable to upset your inner life.

Create a drawing in your notebook with no other hue than the color of the pen or pencil you are using now. Begin drawing without exerting energy or any image in mind. Hover over the page and let your hand circle and draw lines anywhere it wishes to move.

As your hand moves—and you feel great, do not hesitate to write instead of draw. You may want to create pictures or complete a design, instead write. You will discover others will not remember what you did in September after a month or two passes. Why? Your century is expanding faster than your friends' and family's minds can take it in and understand. Thus your miraculous changes or lack of interest in them will seldom be noticed now.

If you find you are writing constantly—even running out of paper at times, think about why you want to know so much, yet later cannot remember half of what you wrote. If you are resting in Spirit and working only on what is delivered, you seldom remember it once you return to your everyday life. Consider that an advantage you wish to promote and such work will appear within the month.

Take your time, but meditate on only one thought now. When it is too hard to retain or repeat your daily thoughts, you are deep in the world we wish you to enter in order to create the proper attitude to Write in Spirit.

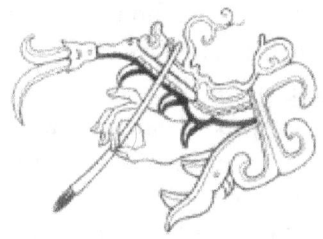

Lesson Five

The time has come when you must decide if you wish to use all of your life when writing or only what you can see here and now. Once you decide to delve into your deepest life and use it to enlighten this time, we can help. If you decide writing like this—without a lot of effort—yet barely able to meditate an hour daily is fine, then it is time to drop out and think more about it.

If you decide it is difficult to Write in Spirit, but something you wish to develop and work with—using all aspects of your life, we will begin working harder on what it takes for you to go deep within and ascend to your highest level of guidance, as well as how much you can use it now.

Take a nice long nap or sit for a long time totally relaxed and you will feel better every time—and perhaps collect advice about your everyday life to gift yourself. Do you believe you can go deeper and deeper and return with even better ideas about what to do now? Can you imagine it—and then write about it? Some do, while others wait for time to evolve—only then opening to see where they are.

To develop your mind so you can leave it behind in order to work on the mundane while writing about another world takes discipline—and it takes time away from being with others. If you are now surrounded by people, forget about moving only as far as the next table or neighbor to write. You will be blocked by their energy as effectively as if talking with them.

When you work outside your home base now, you set up a type of defense system which is effective if no one bothers you then or when you lower your head and appear to be writing. However, if you normally write using a keyboard and wish to write that way now, you will be surprised that what appears is neither wise nor deep enough to study and teach others.

We want you to decide what is worthy of you to write with a pen—and not go back to writing on a keyboard of any type until you must earn a living, run an errand on line, or whatever. Realize and believe you cannot see deep enough within You when your fingers are flitting about. Your mind is not centered within then, it is working for others.

When you write daily—which is required if you wish to apprentice to become a Spiritual Scribe at some point in this life, you may start feeling as though what you write does not belong to you or what you do—or how you work now. You will be right!

If you can Write in Spirit now, or will be by the time you finish this workbook, you may decide you wish to scribe as Ruth Lee might or like other scribes written about in old texts and mentioned on ancient funeral steles found all over the world. You can become a Spiritual Scribe, but it is not easy! Before you can open to such work you must train and be able to Write in Spirit not only for yourself, but for others as well.

We deliberately provide few clues as we hand you mysteries to solve, because you can easily discover how a Spiritual Scribe writes by simply reading the Books of Wisdom scribed by none other than The Scribe, Ruth Lee—and written in a way not very different from how this book is arranged.

Will you want to work hard to become a Spiritual Scribe? You may wish to Write in Spirit so you can claim 'others' told you what to say or 'they' said you are great and can now quote them, but it will not work. This is not how you become great enough that others in need of a spiritual scribe will engage you while here. You must work without any assurance you will one day be called to work for The Lord of All or anyone else approved by your Higher Self.

Always, always remember to dedicate your daily work to that which is holy to you—not what one day will ruin you or cause you to feel the bruises and stings of being rejected by those who can easily see through you.

You are here to explore and develop your inner world!

Since you have new things to wonder about—and doubt, let us assume you are now ready to Write in Spirit. In your notebook write several paragraphs longer than you normally write—beginning with anything you choose to explore more. Do not change the subject until you gain insights into why you want to know more about it.

Write without stop and build a stronger will and the power to work longer hours. If you cannot work sitting straight and tall for at least several hours every day—for ten or more days, who would ask you to scribe for them?

As if this is all there is to consider, think about what you got from this lesson. Why is it difficult to write about what you never knew—or never read about until now? Once that area is explored, you are ready to Write in Spirit!

Lesson Six

As each day passes and you complete one lesson at a time, retracing whatever you did not get while working on previous lessons, do you feel better or are you without any way of measuring your progress? If possible, walk about and look at the place where you exist now and think about it—a lot.

Are you now ready to advance or do you wish to continue the dance of youth and inexperience—moaning and complaining that you do not know how to do whatever and so on? Are you eager to drop all the work assigned and leap into time? If either is you, then you are still unable to understand what you are trying to do here. You may believe you want to write without direction from your brain and so on, but you are not sure or you are not pure in your intent when advancing without serious intention to better your world and the life you live here and now.

Forget what experts say about writing and you cannot write good enough to scribe for others in any worthwhile way, but do not work so hard learning grammar and structure that you forget to be yourself. You may have majored in writing in college and learned how to write a novel or such, but *Writing in Spirit* does not work the same as you were taught. This is not about writing a novel or how to gain faster access to whatever you wish to write in order to impress others. This is about accessing your inner, spiritual life!

Once you can meditate without thinking about what you will write, you are ready to begin an exercise designed by no one of your kind. If ever asked to teach this class, it is not about how to design it...it is about *Writing in Spirit* and how to do it.

Begin by lifting your hand and placing it in your lap or on the desk in front of you. Look at each of your extended fingers and think about how they curl around a pen. Visualize it before you pick up any pen and watch how you feel after having thought it out first. Was it easier or are you self-conscious about your hand and how it writes?

If you feel constrained or unable to feel as comfortable as before, you now know what is happening when you set out to write without feeling it first. Think about it—check it out, then write instead of sitting still until the will to write comes to the surface and you can write without stop for one page or ten. *That is writing!*

You are flying in your thoughts now—not editing and laboring over the effect each word has on another. You are not judging if your work is what others will want to buy or read or have already bought, because that is *writing!*

Notice that *writing* is not the same as *Writing in Spirit*—right? You may believe it is the same now, but once you start *Writing in Spirit* you will realize *writing* is different, and this is not why you write to communicate or how you normally write when preparing term papers or a thesis. Release all work you planned to do or read about for a year or more and order your mind to explore more information and organize it for you now. That is how *writers* write and how you will write—every day explore this work more!

Note: *If at the end of any lesson you have nothing to write—nothing to project through your writing, then rewrite that lesson in cursive script and see if by the end you are writing freely again. If not? Then project yourself into that lesson and reword it until you can write on your own.*

Lesson Seven

Once you can write what you think—without writing it out several times and ripping it up and starting over from scratch, you may believe you are a talent to be reckoned with by many others, but it simply means you can write. You can now sit and place your thoughts on paper in an orderly way. However, you still have to edit many times whatever you write if you wish to publish it or assign work to others based on its content.

When you write, make it great! Do not sit and celebrate life as you thought it was or hope it will be once everyone knows you better. Instead, look within and examine why you talk as you do, or why you never did whatever until now, and so on. If you are poetic and have a great vocabulary, please use it. However, if your vocabulary is meager and you eagerly assault others with words they generally find abusive, ignorant, or without value, please hesitate to repeat it on paper. Be aware your writing will be here long after you think others have forgotten it.

All you do now is without thought about the future—or you constantly think about how much money you will make once you can write without worrying about content or grammar. You will still not be famous or rich—even if you write the most prolific work in the universe—unless you can get across to others that your work is good or even great.

How you advertise yourself will determine much, but today we refrain from telling you how to market your writing. Why? Because it will take you away from your spiritual work and the search you must continue to pursue in order to be able to scribe such writing, too.

Take time to look inside now!

Can you visualize a tree? If so, watch it go into leaf…then lose its leaves and become a tree of a different kind. Please proceed to practice visualizing this now.

As if you now see the tree and believe in your ability to flesh out what it can be if changed dramatically, look at your life now. Change nothing about it, just look at it.

When you lie about your past to another or several others, think about how it changes the way you see yourself now. Do you want to change? Do you wish to say proudly you have been loved, and you wisely used all you were provided by another? Say it now and see how it feels. Once done, proceed to change until it becomes reality.

You can create *the ideal* in your own way now, but it is not going to change once you write and publish whatever as being you today, thus you are encouraged to think little about yourself. Writing is about life…and you are only a small part of the entire being you *really* are. You have much within you now! You can aspire to become and will become whatever if you put in the time—and perspire enough to create the right place for it to grow.

You are who decides why you live as you do. No one on Earth put upon you what you hate, unless you are under age 17 and living with your parents and must obey them. In that case, you are excused for another year or two. Once you can sense that as an adult you are equal to everyone else and can do whatever you want that is legal, beautiful, and will not antagonize others, you will find all manner of ways to excite your mind and believe in yourself—or you will drug yourself until you are unrecognizable by your entire tribe. What kind of mind would drink so much alcohol it could never feel wonderful or appreciate others? What kind of mind would set out to become addicted to whatever is currently used to drug the population into submission and the belief that nothing matters much?

If you want to escape your work or your life and cannot because of obligations you foolishly made and must keep to retain your dignity and prevent harm to others who trust you, develop your spiritual life more and dream less about the world around you now. Once your obligations are settled, and you are prepared to enter your own work of this life or enjoy retirement from it, you can write as if the world required it, but not until then can you develop your work and enjoy whatever you find in the crevices of time.

We recognize that writers are not always liked due to the way they describe life. Also, being honest can lead to being kicked out of your tribe at times, but if it is necessary for you to rid yourself of others or how they believe or appear now, then take it up as a challenge. If you do not believe in shopping as a way to cure insomnia, or believe shoplifting is theft that deserves prison time, you can write about it and seriously discuss the subject, but who would it reach? Instead, we suggest you remember to tinge such thoughts with love—making it humorous rather than condemning others.

As if this is the most serious work you will ever do, write about what you did when you were a child that was so bad your mother cried and your father, if he knew about it, complained he was sorry you arrived in his life. Write about it and see why it is better to think about it with love in your heart—and create a funny story. Let it settle inside your life as something that taught you more than most other events ever did.

Write about you now—tinging it with humor! We will wait for you to complete this assignment before beginning the next lesson.

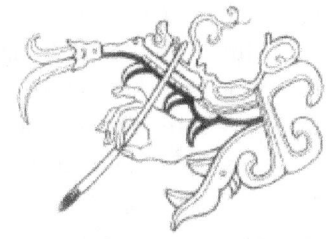

Lesson Eight

When ready to write, do you procrastinate? Do you wait for The Muse to come forward and provide you with inspiration or some other sort of nonsense that means you are not in the mood to communicate anything of use to anyone you know or care about or might ever meet in life? Then this lesson is for you!

Whenever you try to write and feel something will not work, it usually turns out you do not write then or what you write is pitched as soon as it is done. Why bother to write then? Why not do something else? Because your mind makes up excuses and permits you to play hooky constantly—or at least until a deadline is here or gone. Thus you are judged to be incompetent—proving what you have been saying about yourself all along.

Behind the protagonist is the worn-out dreamer and the one who thought this would be easy, but *Writing in Spirit* turned out to require work. You may not believe you are naïve, stupid, or unable to do this work, but it comes to the forefront when you sit down to write and have not used one idea based on your current life or been open to what others have said or written about the subject.

If your ideas are not worth your time, often you cannot write. Your mind reminds you of it, but there are ways to open up and write even when you feel you cannot. Here are several ways to open a subject, write faster—more fluid, or even create a single word that makes it into print:

1. Make a list of things you hate to do and keep it by your desk. When stuck and unable to write, think about doing something you hate. If you are stuck, do whatever is next on the list—no rooting about, choosing something more interesting. You may still be stuck, but at least a disagreeable task was completed.
2. Breathe directly into a paper bag several times—let the carbon dioxide hit your eyes while you think about how great life is now.
3. Immediately read a great book! Have a stack of books beside your desk and beside your favorite chair that inspire you with well-written prose and ideas you would not have considered had you not read about it first.
4. Thinking about how nice it will be when your book is done might result in writing a lot, but probably not. Believing you are a famous writer does not get the job done, either. In fact, it quite possibly stops progress!
5. Look not at the clock! Instead, look at your work, knowing why you write and when you can stop—then all will appear to be impossible or get you writing again. Use whatever works best.
6. You alone know what you want to say, so write it out now!
7. You have a lot of work you want to do, so write about what you need to know rather than show off what you do now or did in the past. Hopefully, that arouses others' interest in your research or inner views. If not, you may not be cut out to be a writer.

Now that you have studied the list, which item clings to you, making you wish you had done it in the past whenever blocked? If none of these ideas help you, realize it is because you are reading now—not writing! How easy it is to think you know everything when you do little but read what another does or advises you to do. Apply these things one-at-a-time, then speak of what works for you and what is of no use. You then know what you can do to get started and what will get in your way and provide yet another way to stall and not work hard.

Can it be writers are designed to moan and groan and feel alone? To write, you have to set aside your outside life in order to delve into what you feel, believe, or wish to reveal about your inner life or the subject you want to discuss. Remember, no one alive knows what it is you want to give, because you are the designer of your work. If you are bored with it, why would anyone buy it?

Be serious about your writing or give it up!

As you think about that line, what bothered you most? Perhaps you thought you would be given a 'golden rule' to measure your prose or you thought all books must prove to readers they are worth their time—and whatever you promised must arrive exactly when expected? Be wise and remember: Only those who write buy such workbooks, and only those who read have made it this far.

This lesson is complete, but to let you go without a writing assignment seems seriously out of alignment with this workbook's intent and purpose, thus we ask you to write about a woman you know well who never listens to you, yet continually asks for advice. Write about her until you run out of ways to help...or help others ignore her more.

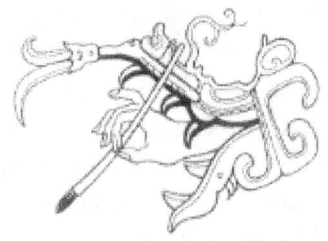

Lesson Nine

Within you—and everyone you ever meet is a story about self and what you lived through, as well as why you do whatever today. Do you believe anyone is interesting enough that you would spend money to buy their story? Would you set aside your life for hours at a time to read about them and what they did? If you say 'No', then forget about writing your autobiography!

You are like everyone else—and everyone else is like you. Who would buy your expose beside family and enemies is beyond contemplation now. Be aware you are living as you read and write—and reading about yourself or writing about how you once lived cuts into your ability to experience an interesting life right now.

When ready to write and you want to talk about someone you know, try to see it on their terms first. Would you want to talk to someone who humiliated or portrayed you without friendship in a literary way? If you say you do not write fiction, per se, but like to use real-life people to populate your work, use your own life.

If you write about yourself—and you usually do when you think it is about another—be kind. Don't try to run over others with bold strokes of insight, unless you are trained to give such advice or make such criticisms. That leaves you with what to write about?

You can always write about how you see life, how you think, and what you believe—putting it out there as being several others' story—or let Spirit enter your mind as Jeanne Beck did in **Writing in Spirit ~ *Jeanne's Story.***

Jeanne was a good writer who broke into greatness by accessing her spiritual source. She published what she wrote when in trance, and it was so valued by others that she became popular and made a lot of money. If that is something you cannot relate to as ever happening to you—because it is nonsense or you never heard of an honest and sincere spiritual person making it big, then your writing is peppered with cynicism and unlikely to be admired by many others.

What about positive thinking helps a writer create works of fiction others might enjoy? It may have nothing to do with popularity, but the writer feels great when the work is done—and probably while creating it. Why not enjoy life as you write?

All you gain from this work and this workbook is what you expect—and a bit more. You cannot get a lot from a work of art if you do not understand how it is done? Many see art and love it at first glance. They never figure out how it was created and may not want to know. You, however, as a writer are a curious person, thus you want to know how others enter into different mindsets, or another life in this time, and write about it.

As you part company with the part of your mind that says it requires proof of whatever before it will write a word and enter the part of your mind that says an artist is not driven by force, nature, or nurture, but by a spirit within that must be heard, you will decide if you want to Write in Spirit or not. You may find you are happier than ever before, because you are now aware there is such a world and you only need to say you wish to enter it to find it. That means you have accepted what?

You and others can write using a computer or other mechanical methods to publish your work, but only the pen pressed down, and the paper accepting the ink, makes you think as you must to Work in Spirit now. You can change and adapt to other ways of writing once you connect and are able to easily write this way. For now, do as we advise and skip ahead of the class that insists on always doing whatever they want.

You are aware by now that this work is different from what you would have created about *Writing in Spirit* and not exactly what you expected based on work you've read by other scribes. This workbook is about *you* in a way that is impossible to describe without talking about things you do not like to mention to others.

This is all about who you are! This is how you live and what you believe—and not to be bandied about by others. Thus, many will write as we advise and never tell you about it.

Why would anyone want to hide the fact they can easily access their Higher Self and write without preparation about subjects of great importance to them? We notice it happens a lot when others are in competition for what they believe to be scarce goods or rare applause. You need not feel that way. You are writing for *you* always, and others may or may not want to use what you write, but you rise and soar based on what you access within You.

People the world over believe writing will lead to great prosperity. Is that why you are trying to Write in Spirit now? If so, go away and stay away until you grow wiser.

This world is not going to increase benefits. There are more and more people working than ever before, but costs could soar and take people beyond the need to have sex and produce more children than they can possibly care about. They may instead use that same impulse to study their lives as lived now.

Why not lay about, smiling and having great conversations with others vicariously? You cannot cozy up to a computer that long, and anyone who seems okay on screen could be totally different in real life. We notice the need to share what you do spiritually is not something many are prepared to talk about or share with others. Is it because they use it to get ahead and do not wish others to benefit from it, too?

Is all of your world in a state of jubilation today? When could that happen—and what event would affect everyone that way? Can you imagine it? If so, enter into that spirit now and write.

Describe how others feel and where it began and how it spread, and you definitely have the premise for a good article or two, but not a great novel. Why not a great novel? Because those who love such works seek lives of desperate and disparate men and women they either despise or identify within their own lives.

If you feel you cannot devise a utopian plot of any kind, think about what you would like to see happen immediately—then extrapolate your feelings and explain your behavior toward everyone around you now.

You can now write—No need to linger any longer!

Lesson Ten

There are ways to open your mind to what lies approximately five feet above what you can see now. However, most people do not want to look up or seek what might be better or appear brighter. If only they would raise their sights now!

Are you one who continually seeks answers or do you wait for others to show you the way? We are now addressing how to seek and let another or several others share what everyone does here. Once begun, you are required to immediately follow through using several different styles before you deny you can rise and use your third eye.

This lesson is easy! It will be so easy you will remember it the rest of your life—IF you are doing work that opens you to what is inside and around your life, yet not discussed much with others. If you wish to discuss this lesson with a friend, be aware you will not keep secret what you did here or honor it as it deserves until you can teach it to others. We work with you here as Teachers of other planes and other spaces, because we contributed work to your life on other levels of time.

Did you sense something new being introduced to you in that paragraph—something that makes you stop and review what you do or perhaps wonder if it is something you too can do soon? If not, you do not understand what *Writing in Spirit* is—yet. Take your time, release this work and let it sit! Do nothing for several minutes...

Did you sit for at least three minutes, or were you unable to follow simple instructions and do what was asked? If the latter, you will not get much done today, so gather your wits and think about what you were doing when this class started. You may as well limit your time spent here now and come back when ready to settle down

If you are still with us and ready to move ahead now, thank all who raised you to behave as an adult or as a sane person might react to that which is given freely with the intention of helping you rise in life and conquer your mind—becoming someone you can easily like, too. You are not to despise others? You will, so do not say such things and then have to lie about it later.

How did that last line work on your mind? Did you deny you classify people or prejudge people based on how they relate to you... or how they look...or the way they talk? You are human and given the ability to save time and not get involved with people who will not benefit you. You do this individually, but use skills and knowledge gained from many others.

Take your time, but describe a woman or man you do not like. Provide details and explain why you dislike them and if there is any hope of ever becoming friends. If you cannot remember such an individual—insisting you cannot describe such a person now, you are lying and we prescribe that you write for an hour now. You will be unable to write for an hour or longer on a subject you devise without finding an honest answer to your questions and what you are trying to hide now.

This lesson is not easy, yet it began by appealing to you as something you would discover when you thought about others within a higher frame of mind than you normally use during the average day. Becoming enlightened or psychic will not make living this life easier—and in many cases it is harder, because you see more easily through veils used to disguise lies.

All is good! With a villain and a theme, mastered by simply describing someone you do not like, add another character to the story. Think about how he or she will react when the villain begins to assert his or her will. Will your added participant willingly let the villain grow as aggressive as he or she wishes or be squashed and immediately put down with nothing lost?

This is your time to work in another life—a life far superior to what you have now. Most resort to writing only about what they know. If you have not been aggressive in weeding out villains and others of a negative mind set, you will not have a lovely story to tell, or you have to manipulate the villain in some way to accept the blame. This is never easy to say, but you are both hero and villain in your story!

It is you who will be blamed for whatever you say. Why? You are writing in character today—and that is how it remains!

If you let go while working on a novel, suddenly seeing the entire scene or feeling the entire plot revealed, is that *Writing in Spirit*? No! However, if you can sit without thinking about anything for a few minutes or even an hour and get a novel given to you bit-by-bit, hour-after-hour, as if you are reading it for the first time—you can say you are *Writing in Spirit* then.

In the event you have nothing to do now, your villain and others having been put away for another day, pray you can rise above all your life and see what you did that was wise and good. Keep that vision in mind until we work another time...

Lesson Eleven

Whenever you feel better than you believe others might feel, do you boast or crow and say so? If so, you are no longer able to do so! You must not say you are observing others and why they do whatever, if you wish to write about it. Writing requires you to observe and then commit to paper your thoughts about it.

What if you never write about what you do in life? Does it emerge when you write about what you honestly believe to be another's beliefs or their life story? You see others in yourself and measure them according to how much you expect of you then. If the other has more of whatever than you ever had, you will be tough on them and expect them to do better. If, however, the other had less and never got as much attention as you did, you will most often bless them and grant them positive attributes, because you believe they are better than you.

Today, work out a stage play. It is to be a play you use to demonstrate your moves and how you improved and did better than those you once thought of as better than you. You will help them grow and develop the way they work today. The protagonist is not another person—just *you* in another's wardrobe and role that day.

You will find writing in a very dramatic way demonstrates your usual behavior. It will be easy to determine if your mood is down or up now. You may deny it later, but if you are crying, you will choose to create a drama now rather than a comedy.

This point in your work is crucial! You have to decide who you prefer: the comic or the one who speaks what she believes will happen or has already occurred. You can chronicle the times as they are now, adding editorial comments on the side as Shakespeare and others tried, but most settle for protesting whatever life did not provide them this time. You will notice this is the most likely way to play out dramas today.

If you usually see yourself as blessed and able to tap into your spiritual work, you do not assume it would be harmful. Right? What if you then meet another who is consumed with the idea that spirituality is doomed or of a demonic intention and so on, would you change? Are you set in your ways, too?

To determine how strong you may be and what you truly believe, write down your beliefs, then let others comment. If you get riled and totally upset because another does not agree with you, then you know you are not secure in that belief or you are unsure if you believe it now. Be aware you will change, however you believe now, once you let another read what you intend to publish during this life.

Why publish works about what you do if you are writing primarily for you and whoever follows you? You may not wish to discuss your life, but *the public* starts diminishing you somehow by saying you are not who you are—so you counter that opinion by writing about your life as you found it originally and how it is now. That is a legitimate reason to write, but what about individuals who have contributed nothing to mankind, and generally are not very kind, yet advertise widely what they want to buy or sell now?

As you publish this work in your own way today, make room in your notebook for more and more research you need to support your conclusions—before you let it go out the door. You may not think Spirit is linked to research, but then again, what do you know about *Writing in Spirit* even now?

While creating lessons for this book, we watched over a class conducted by The Scribe. We noticed many cried and wrote quickly about something they had not expected this life. Everyone who said they were upset believed it was because they were singled out and not blessed—or not supposed to have such stress. Do you feel much like this?

Do you believe you are supposed to have everything you ever need or want taken care of by some divinity? This lesson is not taught by someone who says you should know better than to believe such things, but we do see the need of human beings to teach that you will be blessed if you follow whatever is given whenever, as if it is a test. We do not believe in your need to follow what others pretend is required or necessary in order to rise and feel life is better than it was or you experienced a miracle, too.

Realize now that you are not provided with Guides for any other reason than to steer you away from what would clearly undermine your life for a very long time. If you never follow such wisdom, you have no idea if you are on the clear and easy path today—or in muck up to your neck and unable to clear it away before you leave this field.

When suddenly hit with material that is not what you expected to read or asked to follow and believe, do you generally reject it? Do you hesitate to even read it? Do you go forward and wait until you have absorbed material before making up your mind one way or the other?

At this time, we ask you to write about how you learned to live and who taught you what to do whenever you meet another who is unlike you.

Lesson Twelve

Today you will drop out of your usual thoughts and lean toward fantasy...letting yourself feel like someone else is inside your mind creating a new kind of work or a life you may not have ever thought much about or thought of even once. Let go of reality!

As you kneel within your mind, take upon you the veil of light and kindness available to all who prevail. Now write what others feel. You will not feel it at first, but let go of being upset or nervous—realize only you see what you are doing now. Only you are writing and watching what comes to you alone.

Begin by inhaling and holding your breath for a moment or two longer than usual, then exhale with a sigh—a sigh that cannot be detected as such by others. As you lean into this thought and feel less worried about what you will write, pick up a pen or pencil and write whatever you see in your mind now....

As you sit and relax, believe you are in charge and whatever you write has nothing to do with others. This is an exercise in delighting you and choosing what you would love to do with your life. Write a sentence about what will happen if you cannot work as you normally do every day or two. Describe the worst outcome.

If you can easily assume the worst, what would happen if you were to never do such work again? Can it be worse than what you described or will it blur and not be a worry? Write out what you believe will happen if you do not continue as is and never return to this work over time.

This exercise is about stretching your mind—
not about fantasy!

You may say it is fantastic to believe you might leave your job and never go back, but it is possible; thus not something you cannot possibly imagine. We want you to let go of whatever you are doing at home or school or wherever you are now. Let go and let it be known you will now do something you never did in the past—and all will laugh.

Everyone laughs when upset with others they believe they own, or may be responsible for, or want to control, or get to know better. You must persist with what you wish to do! No one else cares what you think about now, but one day it may be remembered as when you became yourself, or became a writer, or moved out of the past and became another who did much better. Try it!

As of now, your notebook is filled about half-way and you feel like you are not writing much better than when you started—if you are average. If you are *Writing in Spirit*, feeling the power of others lifting you and guiding your hand now, you may say: "This is the greatest work I ever had to do while here on Earth." It is all in accordance with *your* Spirit and if you will let it write for *you* while here.

Lesson Thirteen

When you can write without stopping to think about it, are you *Writing in Spirit* or not? You may be, but probably not if you only started writing like this a few weeks ago. If you only write on weekends and when you have spare time, it may be years before you break down your ego enough to let Spirit soar, but you can do it!

All the work you do now is beside you—not behind nor in front. Why would we describe it that way, because you live in a sideways kind of world here and now. You do not go forward, then drop back, rather you move beyond what you see in your life as going to happen next—then you drop back into a kind of work that makes whatever happen next. You actually work today on who you already are, but cannot describe it to others until it appears in their lives, too.

Does this make sense or are you grasping at ideas to write about and think through now? You need to be able to move up and out of work done to supply your wants and needs. However, such work always leaves you hours to do whatever you want.

Do not believe you work all the time or have no mind of your own! You are full of ideas if you wish to use them, and bereft of thoughts if you use drugs and think only about having fun now. You can be stunted by the synapses not getting enough space and needing to stop work so you can drop out and not be *you*.

If you want a psychedelic type of religious experience, think about it. Think of an iris and a pupil and write about it. Watch your eyes dilate and open wide, then think about entering the aperture and going deep within until you find your room or a wound that is unable to heal, because you do not want to work on it and clean up whatever hurt you there or then.

As you sit and either work on what we suggested or think it is not something you can do, you are stopped from moving ahead now. You cannot make progress, because you are teaching yourself. Who would teach you anything if your mind was closed to all others?

You may find children become immune to the way an adult relates or teaches them about mistakes and how to improve themselves over time, but once a child matures and realizes no one is going to do their work or give them a life they will like, they change and begin paying attention again.

If you are wandering about and tired of trying to Write in Spirit, you are on the right track at last. You cannot make it happen! You cannot write as if you were in touch with your inner life when you have no religious belief or anything you tenderly want to protect from others. You are not reachable, which may be because you do not wish to be taught anything by anyone.

All in this world work on whatever worlds like to do together, but this world you live in today is fading away. Nothing new or different is on the horizon in the way a new world would be expected to arrive over time. Are you now stunted by the way your grandparents prepared the land or did whatever? You have the means and technology to change infinity. You can do much that they could never see and believe, but all now believe in very little compared to the world they lived in then and there.

You do not have mountains of beautiful trees lighting the sky and holding moisture enough that mud never covers the valleys or causes flooding elsewhere. You are victims of your own wants. You want everything you see others flaunt, and you talk as if you have it all now—even when nothing is yours due to buying on credit or dealing incorrectly.

What would it take to create a mountain using the debt load of a country that believes it is the richest one of all now? At this point, write about what you believe a mountain requires in order to rise again and become as great as it has been.

Lesson Fourteen

This is an easy lesson! You can relax, but take care not to fall back into a lapse of consciousness where you cannot see into the future and do what you like. Be prepared! Know all is going to grow and become as great as ever before, because you are the one who will discover how to redo everyone around you!

Writers provide others with ideas or repeat stories another created before them. If you write the way you always write, you do not wish to Write in Spirit and become someone else. However, you will write much the same—even when taken over by your Spiritual Source!

You have been taught to write daily and either do it now or continue to resist learning a new way to connect with your divinity. You either know how to breathe deeply, relax, and enter into a deep enough state of trance to do that or you dance about the pages looking for what you do not have to work on now.

Using only your mind, place your hand on a paper—without actually moving any muscles. Visualize yourself writing—preparing to write out a list of words you think are so lovely and wonderful you will use them all the time. Create such a list in your notebook now...

For a moment your mind lifts ever so slightly as you work to create beauty. Feel it inside! Feel it lift and refresh you in ways you cannot possibly deny, but may try. Why?

What makes you describe a religious experience as if it were something without merit, even though it was mysterious and caused you to feel quite different from what you normally feel? Is it because you are afraid of others? Admit it! Most who remain aloof and resist talking about belief systems are afraid of what others might say.

You cannot write without fear? Then you cannot imagine how wonderful it will be when you do not care what others say or write, because you are too busy expressing yourself. You have to let go—and the time to do so is when you have discovered a way to protect your ego. Line your mind with lead, so others cannot penetrate and make you dread whatever they find there.

Once the inner lining of the mind is in place, rise above it and open to the work of those who live in other plateaus or planes. They know more than you will ever gain from living in this world! Can you see it or are you now fighting with your mind over the concept and whether or not a demon might try to harm you? You have a mind lined with lead and nothing will penetrate it now... Let go and pretend you can soar and become an angel.

Write without pain now!

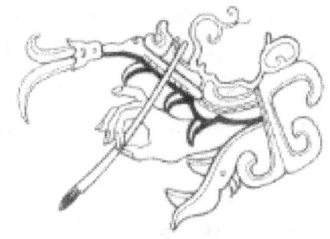

Lesson Fifteen

Do you feel great in the morning? If not, you do not enter into sleep very deeply before the moon is ready to reveal much that is new to you and difficult to pursue. As long as you are alive in this world during this time, you get too little rest and not enough blessings from what is always present.

Who would you be if you could rest, write, and do whatever you like? You would be exactly who you are now. Don't argue about it!

You have to realize that every day you rise when you prefer and pursue whatever you want to do. At times you must be reminded by others about what you said you wanted to do, because some remember your goals better than you. Is that how you live now?

Take time to redirect your mind into a channel where you are totally in charge. You do not get much from others who have about the same mindset as you have now. However, switch the frequency of meeting them and it will change immediately. Do you see the analogy—visualized more than felt? Then you need to keep working with it.

All of your world is open now to many who want to teach and help mankind move above where it has been for years on end—deafening the entire ecosphere with noise and ugly sounds. You may not sense you are bothered by others who talk loud or shout and use as many ugly sounds as they can muster to talk about others, but it does affect your frequency and ability to soften your work so others will prefer it to whatever they normally read.

If you wish to save a few dollars spent on paper and writing implements, do not argue with others in writing. If you teach, you will never be seen as much as your ego would like, but at least you will have helped others gain a higher level of being or understanding, thus able to leave the rest behind.

What if you are a conduit of God?

Is that even possible? Not if you never believed in a higher being than you as able to guide you. You would not be in touch with a divinity! You would be in touch with your ego saying it is *you* who knows more than everyone else in your world. It happens more often than you might believe, but that is not where you are headed today working this way with Spirit.

Relax and release your mind...

Remove it from time...

Think about nothing!

As you remove the usual thoughts and problems you wish to solve, what do you put in their place? Do you think about God? If so, you may be able to leap ahead of many others writing with us now. If not? You can write anyway, but try to gain a lofty way of seeing life in another time or another place and imagine doing whatever alone.

We have not expressed anything that is not equally easy for everyone to achieve, but it is not always easy for you to do work you never heard about before. Thus and so—and here we go—presto—now you know!

You have been told over and over again to write every time you work on a lesson, and may not do it unless told, because you do not like to follow what is described as something everyone should or must do now. When rebelling against your own self, you probably will not listen to others either. What if this is how you *always* react? Then you *always* do exactly the opposite of whatever is asked. You compromise all you read, see, and even believe by *always* refusing to accept anything as is. You want to be sure it is about you—not about others? Probably, since that is why most do not follow directions.

As you move into the new *you*—the one who has changed much since completing the first Lesson in this workbook, you will say 'I didn't change today' or 'I haven't changed', if that is your way; but it does not mean you are right. You will discover that those who believe no one else are usually the most gullible and naïve of your tribe.

Today we will take care of what to say when asked about your writing and how much you did yourself. You are unable to lie once you begin *Writing in Spirit*, because it is communicated across time and space and picked up by your audience.

If the reason you write today is to make a lot of money, by now you are sadly aware it is not going to happen. You have better odds of winning the lottery than making a million dollars writing a novel. Without thinking why you want to write, write out a sentence in your notebook that clearly states why you use this workbook and attempt to Write in Spirit.

The above sentence is the most important thing you have written so far! It will determine how fast you will move toward attaining your goal of *Writing in Spirit* and guiding your life to its highest level of perfection while still here on Earth.

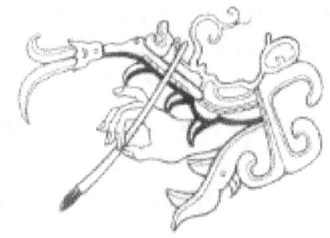

Lesson Sixteen

This is a time when you need to think about how others have used this gift and what they did with it. Why? You then can read and study ways you, too, can Write in Spirit using similar work or wave lengths—as well as how you might write differently.

In the early '90s this Scribe was asked to perform a task for Teachers from another universe, or another world, if that sounds better. Few understood why she was chosen for this work, thus some regarded it as unworthy of their respect. They did not read her work then and do not read it now. However, those who read and study it are changed forever. Is that something you would love to do, too? If so, you are in the right pew!

Today, open a page in your notebook and list books written by someone who was not writing for self, instead transcribing what was being dictated to them. You can find such work in the *Bible, Koran,* or other ancient books of great worth to the human race, but there are many other such works available on Earth. We refer to *The Books of Wisdom* when we talk about Teachers from other planes who employed this Scribe to write and publish great works of art designed to warn humankind of wars and more serious problems to come.

When *The Books of Wisdom* were dictated, they were not given to someone who was incompetent and unable to type or write without stop, rather to someone who had proven her ability over many years as a technical writer—one who never changed what was intended, accurately relaying as directed what was dictated. You may not have had such a career or personally written enough to be asked to scribe for such Teachers, but who knows if it may not happen one day?

You are now writing and studying with a scribe who works hard daily helping as many as possible use what she mastered this life. You may not have learned enough, mastered a trade, hold strong beliefs, or created anything others need, yet you want to Write in Spirit, and may write a great book or work of art if you let Spirit work through you!

Once *The Books of Wisdom* were accomplished and set aside until this Scribe could offer them to the general public for their education and insights, she was given another spiritual gift. To her mind, the gift was so wonderful she never thought about how it would change her life. You may find that to be the case one day, too—or not, but it's always good to know others have had a great life founded on what they wrote.

You still may not realize *Writing in Spirit* takes a lot of work. It does—even though you have nothing to say or do except rearrange the words in order to make it easier for others to read. However, it remains work that interests you, too, because you never lived it!

About the gift The Scribe received upon completing *The Books of Wisdom*? Imagine how Ruth Lee felt the day she sat down at her computer and her fingers danced across the keyboard as if able to think for themselves. She was shocked to see a great title appear immediately—one that amazes her to this day: **Within the Veil: An Adventure in Time.** As time moved forward (as you say) she sat and wrote for about one hour daily—never knowing what would appear or where the story was headed. She was so into the story it never occurred to her that others might not be able to follow it as easily as she did...But that is another story, is it not?

As you work on a book and watch it grow, do you plot it out or let the characters take over the story line? If the latter method is how you write now, you know you are a novelist. But imagine being a writer of technical materials for many years and suddenly writing in ways that cannot be described as dialogue or inner thoughts so much as sharing the same wave lengths with characters then and there.

How can you let go and know you will write a book that will be viewed by some as great, yet not understood by others because of its depth and content? Can you let go of wanting to make a lot of money in order to see what you can achieve and personally gain from writing in harmony with your inner life?

Take Ruth Lee's experience writing books that teach in a 'novel' way and you may want to immediately let go and write as she does—a chapter a day without any editing done then and little changed later when it is published. You would have to trust the material was wise—and you were given a great gift—thus unable to change it to please your ego or make a few more dimes.

Is this why we now share The Scribe's work with you and help you gain such work, too? We cannot imagine how most seekers will Write in Spirit without help! Those who ask for help here and now benefit from her work. How? Ruth Lee channeled this workbook when Spirit said it was time for another class—or time to edit the phrases so they could be followed more easily now.

Once you Write in Spirit you will admire it or scrap it—and not look back, but it is best to let it sit. Let it sit for years if you must, but do not rip up what is given to you when *Writing in Spirit*. You are forbidden to do that!

This is *your* lesson, and it fits in with what we previously delivered, but it is different from what you expected. Now try to write a novel—after you figure out the title!

Lesson Seventeen

Whenever you feel you can sense another—or your other—close by, it could be an illusion or confusion of the mind, not what you seek here and now. Do not believe those who claim there is nothing 'out there' or 'within you' or we are merely air waiting for a day when we disappear. There is meaning to life! You need only check out what others write while in Spirit to see it now—and it could be *you* writing it as well.

Do not work at *Writing in Spirit*, instead let it move within you and come forward. As the depth of your perception of other beings is enhanced, you begin to realize you are not the only one without protection or given much help by others. You will feel it no longer matters that much. You will sense you have the means to work within and answer your own problems and questions—not be misled by those who try to figure you out—*when they are not alive to who they are!*

Take out your notebook now and check to see if there are any problems needing solutions. Can you now answer questions you asked your Spiritual Source a week ago?

To do more spiritual work than ever before without feeling superior, it is not necessary to help others. This work is all about you using what you possess—and everyone else developing as well. It is not about you taking over and helping others do what is blessed by their Guides, too.

You may at some point be allowed to help others, after working out all of your quirks, hazards, and worries, but do not count on it!

To work as a Spiritual Scribe is not something you are here and now working to accomplish—or even close to doing, so take your time and write for days and weeks—even months checking everything that comes to *you* through your work as a scribe to your personal Spiritual Guides. Before you trust your sources, verify!

You may not believe you have Guides of a spiritual type, or you may believe they are angels, animal totems, and other such mediumistic beings, but we are referring to the other *You*, the greater *You* or Higher Self, as guiding *you* through this life. You can now practice asking if you should __(fill in the blank in your notebook)__

Take your time and settle down. When you get the sense a message is ready, write! Write in your notebook whatever you sense or perhaps hear. Let your hand write now without pushing the pen or pencil to create words.

Are you rested—or fretting that *Writing in Spirit* is not what you expected? Do you want to write faster or think the message should be larger in perspective, as if you were Ruth Lee and able to scribe so easily? Try not to think about it! You are not in a competition—and she is unaware you are working here.

You will find once you can write as easily as Ruth Lee that you wonder why you doubted she could scribe this workbook. Indeed, why does she scribe for you when she could be doing her own work—totally unconcerned if you get the message or not?

Now lift your hand off the page and look at your notebook. Think about ways to indicate in your notes when your predictions come true, as well as designating what is about you only—since this could be a new way for *You* to help *you*. Decide if a change of ink color or writing style helps identify predictions... or create check-off lists in the margin when your projections come true or are great enough to talk about with others.

Should you begin following your work in Spirit during the day? We want you to live as you did, but take time now to slip out of it daily and ask your Spiritual Self if you are on the right track doing whatever, or do you need to do something different, and so on.

To get started—
Every time you feel the need to write—Write!

If you want to put all this material away, do it! Thus you heed your intuition, which marks the beginning of a new world in which you trust your way of being *you,* knowing *You* are wise about this life and can discover what you need to know or do now.

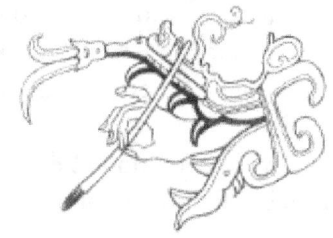

Lesson Eighteen

When you started reading *Writing in Spirit*, you felt it would never come out the way Ruth Lee scribed and told you it would—right? If so, you are defying your mind and not conflicting with her work in any way. You have the model before you and can study her work or ignore it as before, but why not wonder more—doubting what you were told about this life and what you can look forward to now.

The time to work with another who mastered a subject is seldom when you are beginning such a work, but *Writing in Spirit* is not that way. Is it? You now believe you can Write in Spirit and answer your own pressing questions, as well as find answers by simply stopping and quietly working within to see what you get. You are also aware that until months pass and all you write is verified and found to be correct, you cannot say much about it to family and friends. Your spiritual work must be verified as accurate before you talk about it to others!

Take your work home and dream about it tonight. Tomorrow morning write what you saw in your dreams, as well as whatever you noted or wrote about today. Check if your Spiritual Guides confirm what you are doing now, or later if you are tired.

This is your work and not of much interest to anyone else, except perhaps your mother, but even she may not be into it now. However, what helps you become better at whatever you choose to do or helps you memorize what you have to say tomorrow to get a better job or unite with others in a common cause is worth it. Take time to write out your speeches and whatever you need to deliver to others and it becomes easier than ever before to speak in public. Why? You will be speaking with words you wrote from your deepest intellect—and Spirit was involved.

There are enough activities mentioned here and now to keep you busy for the next month, but we are not about to leave this lesson just yet. Take care to write out your dreams, noticing whatever is different from your previous theories or what you now Write in Spirit. Think about the lines of life you will change once you know how to prepare speeches you must deliver in order to be taken seriously by others.

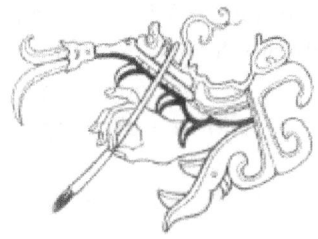

Lesson Nineteen

If you are doing work others vie to do better than you, is this the way to get ahead? Indeed, you will improve whatever you do by *Writing in Spirit*. We know you can always improve, and want to improve now, but what about keeping at it each and every time you sit down to write?

If you are tired of studying 'How to Write in Spirit' and wish to write without further instruction, please do not claim you follow *our way* and Write in Spirit as The Scribe does here. You are unable to know how long it takes to become a Spiritual Scribe, because you have little or no experience working with Ruth Lee or someone like her. She is the only one you may ever know who writes for others as a Spiritual Scribe—and works so deeply in Spirit she cannot remember whatever trance-spired then. She may be the one to teach you to do the same, but it is all about determination and willingness to seek God and perfect what you do first—on your own.

Your work today is to sit back and pray. Yes, write out the words of a prayer in your notebook now and then pray....

As you watch words appear, you may think you should not write out a prayer—reverting instead to thinking, rather than *Writing in Spirit* in your notebook now. That is not what we asked you to do! If you cannot write in your notebook because you are using an electronic medium, you have already lost some of the transmission along the way. It is not easy to write on a computer—maintaining clear and even pressure on the keys—not allowing anything or anyone to disturb you as you work.

Take this work back to your desk at home if you are elsewhere now. Create a sacred place where you can always feel safe and not bothered by anyone while you write. Consider reading **Writing in Spirit ~ Jeanne's Story** in order to gain ways to link with your inner being and save time—or work independently strengthening your mind.

You may not want to believe you can Write in Spirit, which is fine, but if you began this workbook believing you were already *Writing in Spirit* as we teach it here, you are still off-key to a certain degree. It takes time for a big ego, or mind that believes in itself exclusively, to remember it is not orbiting Earth all alone or even alone here and now—but part of a much larger organism—and that organism is not linked to Ruth Lee or another you can see, but to YOU in your entirety. That entirety is like Ruth Lee in her higher being—but not who you can see here and now.

To remember what others are capable of doing—and you are not, is humbling only if your ego is huge and your Spirit is unable to thrive at this time. You can humiliate a human being's mind, but not the Spirit of others. Do not try and you will be spared such attempts on your ego at this time.

This is the end of the line for some students...and the beginning of another way of living life for others. If you want to work on your own—not using this workbook in ways now obvious to you, you can. However, if you wish to ace your life on this planet and get on with your next work or life, try to reimagine what you did when you started working in Spirit and writing part-time.

When time slows and you can adjust your work to fit into any time available to do it, you are a master of dimensional conduct—and can do work others cannot. If you doubt it, check out the work of The Scribe and others who channeled work over the past century concerning the coming end times.

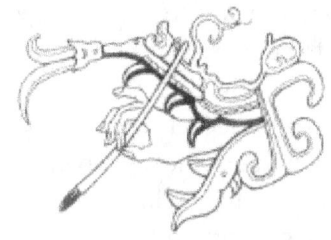

Lesson Twenty

Ready to write now? If you feel strong enough to write for ten minutes without stopping to check the clock, proceed to write about who you are today compared to the woman or man you were when you started using this workbook.

This is not an easy book to work through quickly and never check again, but the average student usually forgets what they did once there is no class they must attend. This workbook does not require group participation that leads to competition with others, nor is it easy to forget its importance in your spiritual development. Why? Because it is a habit or way of working that makes your life more bearable, happier, or easier.

Once you can Write in Spirit, feeling it enter your everyday work without pausing often to breathe deeply and relax, work at it a week or more before attempting to move to a deeper level of understanding. At that time you will want to Write in Spirit nightly—even during the day. We want you to try that!

If your writing is weak, or your predictions are not what you expected, you may not be connecting to your Higher Self—instead it is a being created in another wave. If you drank yourself nearly to death or took strong drugs to get over a disease, or merely became someone else, you may not be able to Write in Spirit. We mention these things as reasons why you may not feel as great as others who talk about their progress in this work. For most people, *Writing in Spirit* is a way to enter and broaden the spiritual life you already have.

Hopefully, you can manage to fit it into your life-style and write daily. If you decide to drop out and leave behind the outside world, remember what The Teachers of the Higher Planes channeled through their scribe, Ruth Lee: *You have to master this life and learn to live with others who surround you, harming no one. You must be able to tolerate all others to ascend…and dropping out in order to experience the life of an elevated scribe of a spiritual type is not advised.*

You can meditate more deeply now! That is a given if you are *Writing in Spirit.* If you cannot Write in Spirit yet, ask your Higher Self to help and provide you with additional instructions on how to increase your power to connect with The Holy Spirit.

There is now a connection between your body, mind, and Spirit, but as time goes by you will favor one over the other, but eventually learn that no matter what you do to the body, it can heal itself—provided you work with Spirit. However, the mind is capable of sidestepping everything you practice whenever you go to sleep—even destroy your aptitude for meditating without assuming a particular posture or mind state first. Nevertheless, all is good!

You may perspire for hours on end over this work or ignite in a moment of time and write more easily. Such works of art could not have been written and be acceptable to everyone who reads them without help from your Spiritual Guides. You cannot disagree that such work would be regarded as enviable and wonderful to achieve.

Take time now to provide your mind with a puzzle to work out or a place where it can sleep and not weep, then write, write, write—until you feel you can Write in Spirit without thinking about it.

Lesson Twenty-One

The day has arrived when you can clear your desk, write a sentence and read it back without feeling you are fooling yourself into believing you can Write in Spirit as taught here. You can write, but always remember why you want to Write in Spirit!

As you dedicate your writing each lesson or session to whatever, you set the parameters for another lesson in life—your life! If you hesitate to dedicate these lessons to higher learning and discovering more about others who are always around you, it is *you* who is not ready to believe you can communicate with your Higher Self and gain meaningful information and an education over the years to follow.

If you stopped attending school or reading great books in order to broaden your vocabulary and increase your knowledge, you will find your work in Spirit is not as great as it could be if you continued to work on improving your mind. Why? Because such work is a reflection of who you are now and what you want to acquire while in this whirl of fire called life in this world.

If you doubt you can acquire an education working on your own at home, you are deeply wounded by impressions another extended toward you. It was done to either harm your progress or get you to work harder. You are who benefits from knowledge gained through your own efforts—not any school or university. You alone need to know what you are here to accomplish—and then do it! Right? Why not work to improve your life today in order to increase your ability to discover why you are here and what you came to Earth to accomplish?

The impression some make when out with others is that they know all they need to know and are ready to fly home or ascend whenever the world ends for them, but it is not that way! You will not be taken from this world without knowing why it is time, perhaps given a bit more time (as a kind of extension) to get it done. Working in Spirit does not shorten your life nor increase your work in industry, but it does save you time aligning spiritually with your humanity.

All is done! There is only one more chapter to work through before you are released to work alone at home and whenever you can escape others elsewhere. If determined to master this work, you will want to explore the area of *Writing in Spirit* more, but you may not be able to figure it out. It may be impossible for you to understand how others write or what makes them write as they do, but you will know why *you* write! That is the gift presented to you here and now.

At the end of each day write a paragraph about what you saw that made an impression on you, yet you said nothing about it to anyone else. This is a good habit to maintain and incorporate into your personal journal.

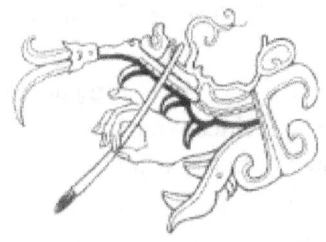

Lesson Twenty-Two

Finally—and for all time, you need to be able to write what is important—not trivial things that develop neither your character nor benefit your fellow man. If you want to be greater than you are, or you are working hard to defeat someone who doubts your ability to write as you do now, be open to a call or summons to Write in Spirit and ready to help others—provided that is why you are learning to Write in Spirit now.

If you heed calls from your inner world, you will notice the most interesting are often hard to figure out until everything else is solved and/or all is done. We strongly urge you to not ask to be called, instead work hard and see if '*a call*' just comes to be.

All of the advice contained within the various lessons provided in this workbook is about the life you can write about now. You may want to share this work, thus hoping to help others Write in Spirit as well as you are—do not! It is not necessary for many to teach a subject The Teachers of the Higher Planes have put out to the world. It helps if you remember that as well.

Take your work to the most worldly players you know today and they may say you are crazy, but you know you are writing better prose than they are—with less effort and more intuitive input channeled into your everyday life. Whatever you do, make sure you feel great. You may not be on the right street, thus miss the bus to your next work, but at least you are out there trying to figure out life.

Now is the time to study **The Books of Wisdom** with an interest derived from having worked hard to write as The Scribe does here and now. You will sense it is easier when you know it is a skill you can develop--if you always produce your best work. If you want to scribe as another might, you will find it is a lost art and no one does it quite the way The Scribe does it today.

How can anyone describe the way Ruth Lee writes and not want to do it, too? Millions know of it, but never thought to try it. You can now work on it if you can spare the time. We realize drive and energy are provided to those who wish to scribe and have the ability to move into their Spirit with skill, but it takes time for you to decide if it is *You* writing or not.

Take your time and write what you intend to accomplish in the next decade or so—and why it will benefit you as well as others—then set your predictions aside in a secure place. Ten years hence see how close your descriptions of life from this point on follow your predictions.

Blessed is she, he, and all who love God—
and wish to scribe!

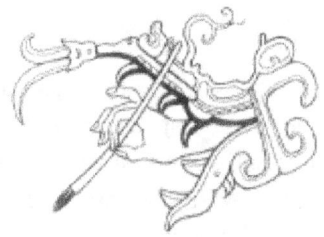

About The Scribe

Whenever asked about a class you took in order to learn how to Write in Spirit, or how you became such an effective speaker or copywriter, you may not be able to describe Ruth Lee or those who created the prose she scribed and delivered in this workbook. For that reason, here are a few clues designed to help you better understand how she normally works as a *spiritual scribe*...

To create this workbook, Ruth Lee wrote in Spirit daily, non-stop, sitting for hours without moving more than a few sets of muscles. She no longer can do this as easily as in the past without help from others, so it is the 'others' you are to describe—not The Scribe.

The Teachers of These times are not the same teachers who dictated or trance-scribed The Books of Wisdom through Ruth Lee in the long ago past. This is a different group--one that can work with you as if you were their sole student. No one will ever write as you Write in Spirit now or will be able to write when you apply yourself to it over time.

The Teachers of These Times is probably the best title to describe 'the authors' of this workbook. They are not individuals as you might imagine or spirits as you might describe such beings to friends who are as ignorant of the work of Spirit as you were when you started working this way with Ruth Lee. The teachers you meet in your everyday life are all of one type, and each one may not realize they are working for you, helping you accomplish what you came to be, which is in their spiritual contract—really!

Your life today benefits others only if you are not upset or being used for purposes unbefitting a spiritual being. You are here to work for *You* and your Higher Self—then move on to another aspect of your *humanity* or what you believe to be another life in another place and time. This will be described in various ways by The Scribe in books yet to be published, so you can get a better feel for why it is not easy for you to be yourself and do what you want to do now.

To do what she came to do, Ruth Lee lived many years with those who used her abilities and paid her very little for these skills, but she believed in what she was doing and always worked hard in order to do her best work while here. That is why she is now the only living scribe of her type. You are welcome to fill her shoes and work as hard as she works for you now!

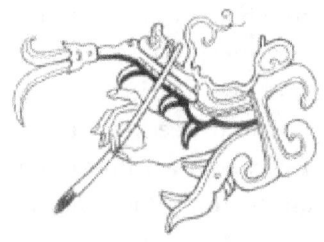

More about Ruth Lee

To say there is a little bit of Ruth Lee in every book she writes is misleading, because it deceives you into thinking—perhaps believing, that her life is an open book you can read and thereby know who she is now and who she was in other lives. We cannot go into her life on Earth, but we can say she has exposed more hoaxes perpetrated by those who exploit faith and the Spiritual way than most who do it as a life work.

Ruth Lee came to work as a *spiritual scribe* via work she did every day of this life. She was entrusted to preserve the work of others who wisely decided how to treat employees fairly, with an even hand. In addition, it had to be legally defensible in the event an occasion arose in which they were accused of bias or fraud. Her job was to say nothing about her work or reveal the identities of those she worked with on confidential matters. Such an advanced degree of loyalty, plus the ability to be discreet, led to this work.

When you are here to work for Spirit, but doubt you can do it, look to Ruth Lee and know it can still become reality. She thought all who proclaimed themselves to be psychic were frauds and set out to discover why anyone would want to work that way. Along the way she found too many were indecent and unfairly treated their fellow man, but she also discovered one old woman after another who passed their spiritual work along to her—work she could not deny was accurate and helped others.

This workbook is not about being psychic or even spiritual per se, more like an education in how to work in a particular way. Why bother to teach you and others how to write or scribe as Ruth Lee does? It was our idea! We want you to see how very difficult it is to Write in Spirit and understand why so few will ever be allowed to use this art to help their fellow man. Not only does The Scribe create manuscripts you can read easily, she has worked for a score or more years helping others live better lives and access their spiritual source. To these few thousand beings she continually sends love and includes them in her spiritual work.

Once you know how to Write in Spirit, will you suddenly realize there are other people who can write as you do? Hopefully, you know that now! If not, you will struggle—perhaps as Ruth did, to discover who is honest and pure and who is a fraud, before you can scribe. May it be easier for you than it was for The Scribe!

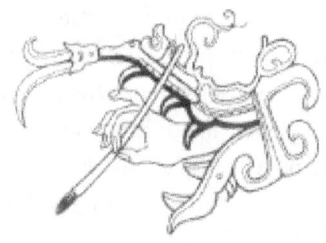

More about Spiritual Scribes

Writing in Spirit ~ *Jeanne's Story* was scribed by Ruth Lee during the first term of United States President William Jefferson Clinton, nevertheless she was shocked to mention Hillary Clinton and The President in this book. Why? She had paid no attention to his election—having voted for his opponent. Let it be known that no work in Spirit such as this is intended to be political or controversial. However, controversy often accompanies such work, as well as being *a spiritual scribe.*

In **Writing in Spirit,** Jeanne Beck becomes a famous writer who has difficulty accepting she can connect with her Higher Self during her everyday work, because she had no model to follow! She had not heard of Ruth Lee or any other *spiritual scribe*, thus she was determined to disprove such writing could be of use to her—let alone help many others. Hopefully, you as a scribe would not fall into such a pit of pride!

Although ***Jeanne's Story*** is enlightening and helpful when learning to Write in Spirit, it is not about her ability to work as a *spiritual scribe.* That development does not occur until many years later when she comes to life again in **Angel of The Maya.** In that delightful work of art Jeanne struggles to accept the fact that much more powerful entities can use her abilities—and teach her amazing things about Earth and mankind. Then she struggles with the duties required to ascend to the work of a *spiritual scribe*, but never creates a book such as Ruth Lee wrote about her. That, too, is something totally different from writing as a scribe of any kind.

If we have aroused your curiosity enough to investigate other works of art by Ruth Lee that teach in amazing and 'novel' ways, please study Mandy, the character most like her. Mandy was introduced to the waiting world in 1995—shortly after **Jeanne's Story** was written. **Within the Veil:** *An Adventure in Time* is what converted Ruth Lee overnight into a writer of novels!

If you are curious about what happens to Jeanne in later years, check out **Angel of The Maya** on sale at Amazon or your local bookseller. It explores Mandy's further adventures with many different characters, including Jeanne. If you are curious to know more about the work of a *spiritual scribe*, namely Ruth Lee, visit her web site at www.RuthLee-Scribe.com

Other Books by Ruth Lee

Novels
Writing in Spirit ~ *Jeanne's Story*

Angel of The Maya

Within the Veil ~ *An Adventure in Time*

Books of Wisdom From The Teachers of the Higher Planes
We Are Here

The Work Begins

The Art of Life ~ *Living Together in Harmony*

Now is The Time

The World of Tomorrow

Bliss is It!

Other Works
The Word of The Maya

The Making of a Scribe ~
How to Achieve a Life You Can Write About

Can You Pray?

We Are All Here to Seek The Way

www.ingramcontent.com/pod-product-compliance
Lightning Source LLC
LaVergne TN
LVHW051849080426
835512LV00018B/3154